THE BLANKET STATEMENT

the blanket statement

D

dedicated to the people who showed me how...

and more importantly

to the people who showed me why it matters.

you can be more than one thing

but sometimes it helps to have a motto,

a steadfast course,

a singular truth,

a through-line that never dissipates

like the forgotten mint in the bottom of your crossbody

from the 5th grade.

but is there really something like that?

an overarching idea to live by,

a thought to constantly return to like

the needed taco on a drunk friday night,

a rooting concept to believe in

and if so,

how the fuck do we find it?

how do we sift through the mess

of things we are told to be

to get to the things we choose for ourselves?

at times it seems daunting.

whether what is more daunting

may in fact be the way to find how we define our character

or the fact that we can be anything we want to be.

it's still our truth to discover,

ours to write in our own dictionary

not something to highlight on the page of someone else's

or fold down the corner of the paper

hoping we remember why we did it the next day.

no

it is intention,

accountability

that fuels how we define our character.

being more than one thing

isn't the negative people try to make it out to be.

being more than one thing makes us interesting,

makes our ideas more diverse,

makes our empathy a wider carriage to hold up

others around us.

so it's important we stay aware

not to define ourselves in the spur of the moment

but to be in tune enough with the things

that define our experiences and in tandem enough

to know how we want to exist in that space.

how to dance through the laughter

and swim through the tears.

how to process

and change

and define ourselves

then change that definition again in our own time.

writing this book...

and why you may either keep reading

or put this book in your garage sale pile

for the spring sale that you'll hopefully empty by fall.

i've said this before and will say it again,

you can be more than one thing.

what defines us is fluid.

it moves, it breathes.

the constructs we create in our own evolution of time,

psychology

and intention

are all woven together,

often like the heaviest of weighted blankets.

in our own vernacular, we ball up the mess

and serve it as a dish on a menu,

listed as one title with a bunch of random things

strung tougher underneath to make us sound appealing.

often, we see or hear a label,

as if it is a goal, that dish that defined

the three star restaurant, a dream to obtain

so that by that world's definition,

we have made it.

this is set on to us.

no,

it's often pushed.

but why do we take it?

why do we put it on like a jacket and wear it

out of the house each day?

all the following words have been used to describe me by

other people, strangers or friends:

dramatic, extra, moody, sexy,

bubbly, energetic, emotional,

passionate, caring, extroverted, empath,

crazy, silly, wild, edgy, creative,

old soul, unrealistic, a dreamer, lazy,

hard worker, flirty, standoff-ish,

and so on.

what all of those words have in common

is that they were chosen for me.

i identify with some of them, many of them in fact,

but others come with connotations,

demonizations,

and worst of all

expectations.

even words that i choose for myself have connotations

that instead of being derived

from the complicated and beautifully constructed energy

that comes from me,

are often connotations imposed by

what surrounds me.

this desired self-definition comes from inside.

connotations are malleable,

molded by how we see the world

and unfortunately sometimes molded by how others

would like to see us rather than who we really are.

what you call me

has a connotation that i may never call myself.

what you call me

may never be a word that escapes my lips.

what you call me

is not your verbalization to say in the first place.

or it's possible we may share the terminology for a brief

moment in time

before we pass in the opposite direction.

some words i use to describe myself:

hard worker, passionate, artsy, creative,

old soul, caring, empathetic,

determined, wild, silly, fun and so on.

how you hear a word and what it means to you

versus how i hear and receive that word

are two different things.

lazy for example...

i am not this.

i often work seven days a week. since the start

of the pandemic, when the world shifted on all of us,

i decided i had to make the most of my time.

i came back home to family, which they fortunately

let me do, and i worked. hard.

i worked remotely full time then got a certificate,

started a second master's degree,

started my own company,

started learning a new language,

wrote and released my own music,

worked on set and created my online presence as an artist.

i am not lazy.

oh, and started this book.

yet, why would someone call me that?

what someone may have seen as me being lazy,

was me in pain.

does pain equate lazy to you?

think about that.

my pain,

was a pain over a history of disconnect from my body

that resulted in a lack of motivation

for the activities that were systemically and publicly

approved as "not lazy"...

by this i mean "active".

the desire to work out, go out, go on adventures

was not in my dna at the time

but i wasn't lazy. i was in pain.

so i pose the question,

why are we so determined to define something?

especially when the connotation comes from the one

defining it, not the one living it.

i am under the belief that it is because our comfort

in a world full of information,

comes from a basic sense of understanding.

the foundation of what something means

has to be defined before we are even willing

to engage with it.

and how sad is that?

to say that we are unwilling to hear before processing.

i will not be able to make a concrete causality

between label culture and self-definition

because to do so would require a wider breath of awareness

than i have in my own existence.

i am not obtuse or vain enough to think my view

can act as a sheet covering the entirety of topics

that may be synonymous to my conversation

or that i can speak on behalf of others

with a thread of a similar moment

but a blanket of different life experience.

but i do think

we start to unveil the ecosystem of our shared reality

by talking.

so i am going to talk now

and hopefully by the end of this,

unpack some emotional baggage,

look at things from numerous angles and maybe

even find a new word to describe myself...

my own statement.

i'm writing this book because honestly,

i want to.

whether for myself or those who can relate,

this book is the shedding of constraints,

pulling off the veils of misconceptions,

thrown onto us as if without them,

we aren't proper enough for the world that holds us

and unshackling the burden

of what we are told for how we should act

and who we should be.

i write this book to celebrate that removal

turned into a new freedom

and to encourage its absolution.

**part one:
time in the
sandbox**

the veil of youth

the gray area

there are bounds that try to hold us in a place of

organization, conformity and structure.

i personally have fought

against all of these things,

including belts which have always

cut into the gorgeous curve under my belly button,

like its a stabbing reminder

that one size should never fit all.

anyone else?

yet, to have the construct of time

be both an adversary and a playmate

is such a unique way to address the idea of conformity.

we all play in the sandbox of our making.

we build sandcastles that crumble unexpectedly,

we team up with fellow architects to make

the best castle ever only to have it be

a mismatched making of two identities

forever struggling to find common ground

and often those works become the latest of ruins.

we slip into laughter and easily into tears when things

don't go our way. time tells us

how much longer we have until the sun sets

on our sandcastle and we must wait

until morning to see how it withstood

the waves of the night.

we are told so often that time isn't our friend.

gray hair comes to mind

as a day to day reminder of time.

i officially have some gray hair now by the way

(takes a bow *thank you very much).

yet, i don't see gray as a negative.

i see gray in the light it deserves.

gray is an open space of blended ideas.

the "gray area"

can be beautiful. it can open conversation

to new bounds, dip its toe

into the unknown and pull together

the molecular bonds that once seemed so severed.

gray space allows perspective to shift

and to shift again,

for creativity to find new avenues

through the labyrinth of our minds.

why can't time do the same?

time can allow us to untangle

what we once saw as forever melded into our scars.

we can use time to learn the depth of our feelings

instead of accepting them at surface level

for someone to scrape off the next day like dry gum

on the bottom of your shoe.

time can teach us to turn our love inward, towards

the intention that drives us.

time can also show us how to engage with the outward

and make the things we do truly matter.

none of this is simple.

if it was, i would have finished this book with the word

"fuck".

don't get me wrong, i'm one of the most nostalgic humans

you'll ever meet. i still cry during many childhood films.

my middle school self felt it and still does

during many a movie musical.

i remember people asked the question

"who would want their life to be like a musical?"

i was the often rare "i do!".

my "yes" wasn't because i planned on serenading my

school crush in the hallway the next day

and wanted someone to push play for me so the music

would blast down the inaudible static of the

middle school hall speakers.

it was a "yes" because i wanted the raw emotion

to flow naturally, a lack of restrictions to limit my feelings

that so often got in the way.

especially in middle school.

everyone sees high school as the worst

but let's be honest. it's middle school. all the way.

needing a release of emotion,

connection to the idea that anything is possible and the

hope that our identities are ours to define

and that our similarities matter more than our differences…

sure is a good message to grow up on.

the difficult thing to recognize isn't that we are aging

or that we sometimes feel at odds with time,

it is that we have a choice

of how to play the game with it.

do we accept time as an enemy

or do we embrace time with an imperfect hug

and jump hand in hand into the sandbox?

the horror of middle school hormones

riposte to my identity

words fly out unable to catch

them in the sweaty

palm of my growing hand.

through chewed-off fingernails, they slither

as if through weeds of caution, yet

no blade strong enough

to stop the momentum.

my identity at the offense

it unleashed a fury of reciprocated judgement

to the verdict, thrown onto myself

just moments before.

and yet, before those words

hit my opponent,

i feel another leaking

out of my chapped and bleeding lips

with no one to catch it,

before they mark me forever,

uncontrolled and at the whim

of my body's pre-teen hormone battleground.

the told taboo

one of the first things we are lied to about

is the idea that a period is shameful.

to bleed is to hide.

to exist is to be stowed away.

the first way this is done is by separating young people

into two groups for sex education.

this already defines one group as different, othered

from the group that doesn't have

the burden of blood.

this persuasion that we are different

due to the act our bodies begin

before we even know who we are

is false.

and yet, we are told this over and over again.

to leak when on your period is terrifying.

i would wear extra layers around my waist to prevent the

smallest infraction from being seen.

we are told our period is an excuse.

then a problem, an inconvenience.

who picked this to be the taboo of the thirteen year old?

shouldn't we be worrying about the things we can control,

rather than the natural evolution of growing up?

does facial hair come with as much shame?

does height,

a lower voice,

maturity?

things that should exist as we grow but shouldn't

demean us to lesser than…

i wish a period was one of those things that comes

without connotation

and should only make us more engaged

with the new phase of life rather than entrapped

into the loss of a previous one.

i got my period early. it also goes

very well into the theme

of time because time is associated with a clock,

ticking down towards "fill in the blank here"

for whatever it is for you.

for women, it is often put on us that we have a clock

to have children. there is biology at hand of course and i do

not dismiss science but i also think that when we hear

over and over that we have limited time

to find love, to have a career, to have kids…

well no wonder women feel this pressure

because missing out

seems societally unbearable.

i do not want kids. i've been told over and over and

over that i will change my mind.

when i'm told this, i want to tell that person

to fuck off.

telling me i have toilet paper on my shoe,

sure!

tell me that.

but telling me i will definitively change my mind

on how i want to live my life,

absolutely not.

or telling me that i will regret not pushing something out of

my vagina?

nope.

what happens is women are told to hurry up.

or they are told they'll change their minds

because it's only right or natural

for them to want kids.

i get overrun by rage when i hear this

because many times, people don't know the reason why

someone doesn't want kids and then

i feel sadness

that they didn't think to ask

and that no one taught them they should.

the idea that there is a reason,

a sentence to explain

or a statement for why you feel that way,

never crosses their minds.

as if all the people who chose not to have kids

simply forgot to think about it or said "eh"

and walked away.

they don't know.

but yet, they have the audacity to tell someone

what they will want in the future anyway.

for me, there are many reasons.

yet, i do not gift those who never asked

with the honor of telling them because they seemed to

believe their right to dictate for me was of more

significance than my own choice.

and i will not reward that behavior.

when i got my first period, i wasn't super surprised.

my boobs were c cups around the age of 13

so you can guess how early they started to show.

what i remember most is this fear of showing,

of being seen such as an accidental period leak.

now that is not something someone wants but why

was the fear so brutal that is would make me cry

if i had an incident at school?

we are so torn into this heteronormative viewpoint that

women deal with periods and men can be grossed out by it

because they don't have to deal with it.

what happens is we extend that mindset

and women become the reciprocating entity of jokes,

embarrassment and fear.

not to mention that this approach is a conversation that

then excludes a gender fluid society.

i've been made fun of more times that i can count for my

body. once, in a high school library.

i was sexually harassed for my boobs being... well bigger.

i was asked if my mom also had big boobs.

now, i did not feel unsafe in that moment but honestly,

i think i was too naive to understand

that fear was an option for me to feel.

i'm not saying i was in danger of further harassment

because i was relatively safe, but i did not have the mental

capability of understanding that this exact situation

a few years later could have had a different outcome

because rejection is taught to have a defensive

response out of men.

rejection is a word put onto women as their fault,

not onto men as their responsibility to handle well.

when my sexuality was water cooler gossip years later

and i realized to the extent

that i felt i had lost control

of how my body and sexuality were described,

i felt meaningless, empty,

unimaginably lost

for control over my own being.

it was like all the other things i had done...

the work, the bonding, the listening

to other people's feelings were erased,

stricken from the record.

even my own jokes at my sexuality and my brazen attempt

to bring healthy sex conversation into the fold

was turned onto itself,

reframed as a label and connotation i did not recognize.

i don't mean that i was perfect.

who is?

yet, i still had a whole catalog

of good things i had done.

when my personal relationships became the cover story,

all of that prior time became nulled,

chiseled away,

non-existent even to the people

who supposedly knew me best.

that's when i began to understand that defining women

by their sexuality goes so much deeper

than who had sex with who.

it unravels the foundation of one's purpose,

fueling a need to give sexuality a higher percentage of

importance in our net worth.

in my pie chart of what i define

as my self-worth, sexuality is not close

to the largest slice of the pie.

love, family, friends, passion, creativity, identity...

all take up more space

and let's be honest, my chart

would be in some unknown shape,

because well, we're more complicated than a pie chart,

aren't we?

i want to be a grown up

i call myself a workaholic

holding the importance of my work

in hand with tender care.

as a creative, my work often seeps into my every day action,

my mood is followed by a song,

my emails followed by poems.

i am proud of how i use this term to define myself.

i am proud of my hard work.

we are asked when we are young

what do you want to be when you grow up?

as if "grown up" is a definitive moment to achieve

as if once we have grown up,

we are done

and can dust off our hands

of the hard work we did on the way there,

forever allowed to stay in place

and rest on the idles of comfort.

growing up doesn't end.

that's another lie they've told.

the next lie

is more of a misconception,

a reiteration of a question

that should be presented in a different way,

rather than the current ask

which limits the array of answers,

which curbs one from etching

into the expansive landscape

and approach the ongoing, sapphire sea.

what we want to be is often answered with nouns,

careers and passions that are a course

of study,

of time,

of hard work.

a doctor,

an engineer,

a rock star,

a president.

all wonderful to imagine,

to pursue and to believe in.

yet, we also don't answer the other half of the question.

"what do we want to be?"

should also be asked as

"who do we want to be?"

i am a proud creative, yes.

yet, also to be kind, empathetic, and caring

are goals to be when i grow up,

to work towards as entities that deserve the time of practice

and the respect of acknowledgment,

not to be assumed as easy or inconsequential.

"what do we want to be" can change,

evolve,

grow,

push past our now

and into our future.

by growing, we allow all of the present

to be absorbed,

metabolizing into the future

through thought

and reflection.

so what do you want to be

when you grow up?

and who do you want to be

while you're growing up?

grown up... no, growing up

why do i care about all the things i can't control?

i never fully understood it but yet, i sit

in the agony of anxiety more than i desire,

waiting to find a rationale to the moment so that i can move

on and live in the new phase of the evening,

forgetting the old and drawing a line between the two.

not that it is ever that simple.

a line. it's never linear like the spine of a book,

but rather the line in the sand,

muddled by waves,

footprints and the imperfect nature

of the creases on our hands.

so why do i care?

i've sat in rooms, for hours, and worried about one thing

that happened outside the building on the way in.

i can't control it.

yet, i worry.

i think it has to do with insistence.

where we spend our energy controllably and

where our fears dictate the rest to be spent,

illuminating us to the harsh light of what we must face.

if i sat and wrote down everything that i worried about,

this book would be quite boring.

it'd be a mess of hyperbole and manifestations

of anxious energy.

that's not productive.

yet, i still care about the things i can't control.

it's a skill to let go, to forget or unwind

the tension we build around the moment,

hoping to block it out of our minds but rather

we enshrine it in a protective wall of disdain.

we protect the things we are frustrated by,

allowing them to set up a home in our minds

rather than be flushed out at the next opportunity.

they sit in a large chair and take note

of what else fuels their existence:

pain, disconnect, or uncertainty.

they latch on to it like a ladder rung, pulling

themselves into the forefront of our decision making

and that is dangerous.

it's not easy to stop

nor should it be.

that would be remiss as the true power these anxieties have

over the day to day of our lives.

but we can hope to tell them no.

acknowledge our needs outside those shrines

and focus our energy there instead.

never easy.

no one should tell you it is easy.

they are wrong and wrong to say so to you

but what you chose to enshrine is up to you.

build the walls high around your empathy,

trust, hope, love

and anything that exudes the best of you.

care.

care about the things you want

and let it overpower the things you don't

want to care about anymore.

part two:
untangling the web
(of lies we've been told
as women)

the veil of body

sex

if you're related to me, you may want to fast forward.

just waiting until they've done so effectively and won't

accidentally see a few words that may change their

perception of my sock drawer.

just kidding!

(kind of.)

at first, i wasn't sure what to include regarding this topic.

did i really want to share this information

with strangers or friends or family?

or was i just scared

due to the inherent shame

that is put onto us regarding the topic of sex.

am i to feel that shame in my own book?

where else does that shame creep in,

slithering through the unwanted but appearing anyway

with its fangs sharpened?

my own sexual experiences?

my work?

my friendships?

honestly, i'm not sure i would recognize the shame

when it does show its face

out of the pure shock or lack of preparation to face it.

so i often think,

how have my experiences been shaped

through the lens of this shame

and why can't i seem to remove the mass of it?

i think of my experiences and one comes to mind first.

i had some of the best sex right before grad school

(or at least up to when i wrote this chapter).

i think we often assume great pleasure

comes purely from great technique.

rather, great pleasure

comes from an intimacy that is not mechanical

but emotional and often transparent.

i've never fashioned myself a casual sex kind of person,

just not for me yet,

i found myself in this kind of relationship

that was not committed yet, also respectful.

i'm not saying that's what made the sex great.

but i'm not saying it wasn't.

so what does make sex good?

if you're related to me, and haven't fast forwarded yet...

i encourage you to do so now.

what makes sex good

and how do we know?

some of you may think we obviously know

if the sex is good or not

but i ask you to really think on it.

there are times i've felt pressure

to be turned on or in the mood and i think why?

why is it my job to feel that way?

who told me it was sexy to be that way

and why the hell did i listen?

"sexy" is what we each define it to mean.

what i find sexy is different than what someone else

finds as sexy so why would i feel the need

to act or be sexy in a "conventional" manner?

i love reading books on the human body on public

transportation especially books on the female body

or sex. it fascinates me how many people do a double take

or look at me like i just took a seat on a public bench

in chaps

which i definitely saw someone do one time

at a stag do in scotland… makes you wonder

how often those wooden bar chairs are cleaned.

just saying.

what shocks me is that it is a human experience.

learning more about our bodies makes us more

knowledgeable, not promiscuous

which has a fucked up connotation of its own.

i would also like to redefine the experience

of "losing one's virginity".

because it is that,

an experience.

the term to "lose your virginity" often applies to,

yes say it with me, women.

women lose their virginity and men have sex.

again, women lose and men have.

have is a possessive term so men get to take

and women must give?

why is that the lie we are told?

lose... no, experience

i experienced sex... experienced sex on a lofted twin bed

which anyone who has lived in a college dorm

knows what i mean.

yet, as i became more aware of my physical existence,

the space i take up or the space i've been

conditioned to not take up...

i realized i had built walls around sex.

the immediate fear i would adopt like that weighted

blanket, it would sit on my anxiety

like a pressure cooker waiting for its moment.

i'm so acutely aware when i feel frozen in fear.

the presence pinpoints the spot between my brows

so it's always obstructing my view

of what lies ahead.

i've been in situations where i'm looking at someone and

think which path do i chose.

the next thought comes even more intensely,

crashing onto me like a wave i can't control.

that question is how do i take the "no" path?

the word that i use is how.

i can't just think what i don't want

but how i am going to explain it

as if i must explain it.

i want to tell my path,

not go to its defense.

sex can be so beautiful.

when someone cares and the expectations

go out the window, along with the vocal ecstasy of

encouragement and validation,

transparency becomes euphoric.

in these moments, the mind can relax

so rather than worry, i should just feel.

is that achievable more often than not?

in these moments, my body answers a language

i cannot speak.

it knows touch the way words are entranced in my mouth.

the body knows more than i do, it's pleasure

an honest reaction of passion and safety,

comforted by the tracing fingers

of someone i love.

yet, it's my body's choice

to move,

to breath,

to hold on to the ever growing intensity

that seeps through my nerves.

because it knows pleasure is a gift.

pleasure is at the hands of its maker

and those hands know what they are doing.

food, fear and shame

prior to my eating disorders, i had lost a lot of weight while

working with a nutritionist.

i learned i was allergic to gluten and worked

to restructure food in my day to day.

this was senior year of high school.

the summer between junior and senior year,

i had breast reduction surgery.

it was something i really wanted and had many

many discussions about

in order to get it done.

now, my boobs are still big but

manageable for this five foot lady.

all of these decisions were about reforming

my experience in my body, wanting

a better understanding and yes,

some kind of control.

i had started a journey of understanding my body, making

choices that were about long-term health and goals.

i lost weight, started a new high school,

started dating, finished college applications, had a fantastic

senior year, started at the college of my dreams…

then it came crumbling down

like the sand castle that can't support itself.

when i started college, i put on some weight

as anyone can because it's college.

it's a time of expression, fun, hard work, learning how to

manage your schedule for the first time.

gaining weight is normal.

yet, there i was, clothes getting too tight and

my confidence shaken.

i began to find ways to compensate, buying a lot of

"healthy" foods such as granola in which,

i would over eat it,

walking every day for lunch to a salad bar

but also buying bags of "healthy" chips

to give me the carbs i was craving,

doing take out when i wanted it and buying two meals

worth to save for later...

which i never did.

all of those choices were rooted in my fear,

something i couldn't put my finger on at the time.

now, i have a better idea of what it was.

fear that gaining weight was losing control,

losing control of the future i had planned for myself,

losing control of the idea that i was enough,

losing my sense of sexuality and confidence.

i started college a week after graduating high school.

my confidence was at its peak, quite literally

and when it came crashing down,

i wasn't sure how to slow it's momentum

enough to save all the work i had done on myself

before it was demolished.

but slowing it down wasn't the problem, was it?

listening to it and recognizing the emotion was the

problem. i couldn't do it.

i didn't know how to address what i was feeling

as that, a feeling.

rather i tried to redirect it, shift it

more comfortably from one shoulder to the the next

as if it was a tote bag i'd discard at the end of the day.

because i feel that this book is about honesty,

questioning our perspective and growth,

i won't hide pieces of this story.

i started binge eating and by thanksgiving

had become bulimic. in my story,

i'm fortunate,

because i figured out an escape plan

but that isn't always the case.

my resolution was to get out,

run,

crawl my way

into a safety net of my own making.

it was a constant renegotiating with myself

over how i would get rid of the feelings

that were ever present in my day to day.

my sleep, my mornings, my creative time

were all being taken over with this

immensity of doubt and shame.

it was so well orchestrated in my mind.

all the pieces that needed to come together

to turn me into someone i didn't recognize,

did.

anxiety, depression, ocd... it overran my story

with its deepened tread.

i don't want to say that i let it happen

because there is no light switch for these things

but i did encourage some behavior that called to them

like a welcome home mat,

laying at the doorstep of every engagement i had.

rather than trying to push them away or persuade myself

to do the thing i didn't want to do, i sat in pain.

not laziness, pain.

since then, i have worked to acknowledge

the tendencies, but as people will tell you,

it isn't that simple, right?

it's not about looking one direction one day

and another direction the next. it is about looking

at the whole picture and deciding how to engage in it.

i work with my anxieties and recognitions now

to process how i feel rather than hide it.

it's an ongoing decision making process that often

includes decisions made for me by these feelings

but i have chosen not to fight them anymore,

not to give in to the ideas i've been told to just ignore,

but rather to see and hear them for what they are,

a part of me.

the me that is able to run a company,

write music, be a filmmaker and write this book.

that is the shedding of the veil of the body,

not to pretend what's inside isn't going on,

but to accept it's presence in your guest room

and learn to live together.

to be better than they want you to be.

to touch

the are many things,

things i dream

i sense, i hope

that would awaken

my body into its own.

i'm told to behave one way,

that its the best way to attract what i want

but is that what i want?

i want something,

something that calls onto me a freedom,

an expression,

but so often i'm weighed down by the things

that i feel compelled to do,

compelled to explain,

compelled to defend.

it's exhausting

rather, i'm exhausted.

i want the sense of ecstasy on my skin,

a revelation of pure mindful freedom

that only comes from trust

and pleasure coexisting

in its bonded form.

the things i sense are palpable

but the things i crave are hidden

waiting for their moment to shine

and that wait may be longer than one hopes.

unless one is willing to explore to find it.

do we wade into options?

or do we try,

try it,

try it again so one day

we are able to know what we want

rather than hold hope for a feeling of certainty

as if it will slap us across the face with a sting of truth.

to tell what i like,

to say this is what i want from you,

this is what i want you to do to me...

why does the exertion of energy to say what we want

feel greater than the energy to do what someone else wants?

the equilibrium stripped of its logic.

how long does it take me to feel the things i feel?

does one need a few minutes and a cigarette

or a week and a dose of patience

to settle into the reality for which they know?

is it confidence

or illusion?

playfulness

or detachement?

it can't be as simple as one word

but rather the connotations,

realities,

implications within

so i can say what i want.

it's a frozen ice bath the next morning

pouring down the searing skin of my neck

telling me i should reflect on the night before.

who put that ice there?

my sense of duty,

my sense of shame?

whoever placed it there is a cold bitch

and yet quite often i do it to myself,

chasing to engage in a shaking vulnerability

rather than accept the closed expression of desire

from the night before.

to unveil that within myself is hard.

it takes patience of my own self doubt

allowing peace within pleasure.

there is no shameful walk.

i'll just walk now.

sparkle puzzle shoes

i own a pair of shoes.

they are heels with bedazzled puzzle piece shapes

across the straps and heels.

you might ask why someone would buy puzzle piece shoes?

i ask why wouldn't you?

i think we often feel we have to conform or buy

the standard thing to fit in.

a middle school phase comes to mind.

another example is work attire for women.

why has women's wear often been such a problem?

i think of how girls in school were often told what they

couldn't wear. we couldn't wear shorts

that were shorter than our fingertips, tank tops

that showed our bra straps and yoga pants

became an issue at one point.

all of those things have in common

the fact that they could pique the interest

of teenage boys, making it our problem

to not distract them.

why did no one say "hey don't stare because

her bra strap is showing".

when did it become our problem

for them to keep control?

this becomes a thing during the age of middle school,

as we grow and our bodies change,

a biological thing.

yet, at this time, instinctively women are told to hide,

to adjust,

to make men more comfortable.

we all remember our first kiss or that high school crush.

hormones run rampant maybe?

sure.

but being pulled over by teachers

in front of the whole cafeteria because your bra strap

is showing or because your shorts

don't extend past your fingertips...

that's not reigning in bad behavior.

it is teaching it.

teaching shame.

it teaches girls to be embarrassed

and even more so by doing it

in front of other people.

it puts on display the idea that you should

be embarrassed when you show your body.

your bra strap shows, you should be embarrassed.

shame sets in with the most simple of physical things.

not to mention that everyone is different.

our bodies and our minds are all different.

what might look like shorter shorts on someone

aren't on another person.

so should that first person

be shamed simply because they are taller?

does a comparative proportion come into play

where we immediately compare ourselves to each other

to see who can get away with existing?

existing as we are without such embarrassment?

i remember in early high school, thongs

were discovered by many.

i love a good thong.

but in high school they were an idea of self-discovery,

of growing up and

becoming a woman.

across the rows of lunch tables,

i remember seeing thongs peaking above jeans.

it was such an obvious and public concept of femininity.

thongs are often associated with women being sexy, right?

the age we become aware of our physical presence matters.

yet, this is the same time,

when we are pulled in front of people

and told to go change.

so presence

becomes tied in with shame,

manifesting in a constant self-ridicule

of existing as you are.

you may think this is an over exaggeration,

but i assure you it's not.

how we see ourselves matters.

and when we are told how others see us first,

through lens of sexuality and shame,

we internalize that in the process of self-discovery

for years to come.

my body is not to be shamed.

i now often wear clothes where my bra strap

can be seen or even better,

the whole fucking bra.

july 1st, 2022

on the upcoming celebration of freedom

i reflect,

not the expected long weekend.

how can i celebrate?

how can i pretend that i am on equal footing,

that my steps make the same indentations

of my male counterparts,

that my allies are seen,

or heard,

or given rights of their own.

how can i celebrate?

the stages of grief show up in their own patterns.

like the woven knit of a blanket,

some threads more prominent than others.

i skip denial

and go straight to tears.

real streaks down my face

overbearing my dry complexion.

i pause at anger

for i don't want to enter it yet.

i need to mourn or else i won't feel the weight

of how it hits me like an unseen fist in the air.

once i enter anger,

she greets me like the friend i needed

embracing my deepest condolences

into the outpour of fury.

i won't bargain.

my rights are not for sale.

depression is a constant.

the waves of it will hit me when i least expect it.

overbearing when i am settled neatly

sunbathing in the sand,

sweeping me out towards

an unknown that has been constantly

proposed as a void of fear.

i will not accept.

so rather than celebrate a freedom i do not have,

i will celebrate the rights i do have

so i can fight for the rights i deserve.

anonymous

do you see me?

i'm sitting here, across the way

token in hand for the ride that has yet to begin.

i'm the one behind the curtain of glitter

encompassed in hard work, motivation and silence.

do you hear me?

i don't pretend that you heard that sentence.

it was well crafted but the pen didn't reach the paper of

your peers. do you want to see me?

i don't think you do.

rather than expand the horizons to an entrancing glow,

you limit your bounds to your own extremities

and no further.

but how does that shine,

through a misty light of indifference?

i shine in many realms.

the lights through the dusty beam on a black box stage,

through the warm and wet morning air

because i see shine as

the anonymity of our pride.

by giving ourselves to the bigger picture,

the growth of shared experiences,

we shine brighter.

we are brighter than the internalized needs.

we need, we feel, we want for ourselves

and have the empathy

to need, to feel, to want for others as well.

my anonymity has been seen before

through middle school halls of light wash jeans

and lack of vintage boots.

through high school halls of makeup

and yoga pants.

the distinction of my expression

often clothed in words that are just on the cusp

of what is expected of us in an imagined "normal".

all the words that put us on the edge of that acceptance,

putting us on the rocky cliff of the valley of people that are

told they are safe.

you know what else is on the cliff?

a view

of the expansive growth of earth's precious landscape,

unseeable forces blowing moveable inspiration through

sweeping grasses

and across colossal waves,

through arid expanses

and up to the unreachable summit.

on the cliff, i see all that is around me,

all that can be dreamed for the horizon

is not definitive

but rather an ongoing entity,

forever reaching,

forever growing,

forever in sight from the edge of the cliff

that isn't a cliff of "normal"

but offers so much more than normal.

balance... no, see-saw

i've learned to hate the word balance.

balance has always been told to me as a goal,

as an ideal.

i struggle to see it that way because i don't think

anyone is balanced.

we are all very smudgy humans.

there are other words to replace the word, balance,

and that is for you to decide for yourself.

i won't tell you a word that defines you.

balance brings to mind a see-saw

as if two acts must perfectly balance each other,

never outweighed.

balance should be about evolution,

not formula.

balance should be fluid,

not lifeless.

balance should be nuanced,

not concrete.

i note all these things with the intention to say that balance

isn't balance.

balance is the web we make full of choices, lessons

and emotions pressed together so tightly

that they form as one.

it is an expansive entity, stretching

its limbs into the widest reach of our limits, testing

ourselves when necessary and embracing

ourselves when deemed right.

we must know how to adapt, to overspend

on energy when needed for a friend and to reign

in emotion when cautious.

that isn't a formulaic balance.

that is responsive and textural.

balance isn't balance at all

and maybe it shouldn't be.

rules.

what are the rules of relationships?

i don't think there are any. we are told

time and time again how we are supposed to act.

like human interaction is placed on a gold platter

and you simply pick the outcome you want.

it doesn't work that way.

we know this.

yet, we teach the opposite.

we tell each other to be kind,

say thank you.

how about stand up for yourself?

where is that headline?

so clearly we are here to dig into the rules

of relationships and why we should break them.

back in my days of undergrad, i had this relationship

with this guy. vague, i know, but keeping

private things private. although i'm about to tell you some

sexual details so maybe not that private.

oh well.

i had gotten out of a bad relationship

and didn't want to date but wanted someone

with whom to enjoy my time.

i found a guy.

smart,

cute,

sweet,

wore the best glasses ever.

anyway, we got together.

this was at the age of 22.

so we kept this up for a while and then

i got my acceptance letter into graduate school.

i was going to move.

i didn't even question my relationship as part of my

decision to move into the next chapter of my life.

we weren't dating to meet each other's parents.

that was never the plan.

we chose how we constructed our dating experience

and that worked for us.

i remember a moment we had though.

the apartment where we had once been intimate

was now empty.

the studio apartment lit only by the northwest

d.c. streetlight outside.

i put blankets on the floor, pulled from a bag of my last

few things to leave the city

i'd known for the last three years.

we knew this was it.

yet, that wasn't the point.

the point was the moment.

i didn't panic over leaving.

i wasn't overwhelmed with the sense

that i was giving something up.

for the first time, sex and a relationship

didn't feel like a loss. it felt like a moment.

and now a moment i would write in a book, who knew?

that moment felt out-of-body.

the euphoric ecstasy and the physical exhaustion

left me with a true bliss that i could take with me

when i moved. i wasn't leaving it behind in the studio

apartment on the top floor.

i was bringing it with me.

when he walked towards his car, i could see him

from the window. i sat on the window sill,

surrounded by emptiness...

a cleaned out kitchen and a few

packed bags in the corner.

then, i saw him look back up at me.

it crossed my mind

that we maybe meant more to each other

than we realized.

still, it wasn't sad... it was freeing.

i was walking into a new chapter,

having this experience wrapped so nicely.

it wasn't wrapped perfectly.

that's not even a thing.

it was just wrapped the way i wanted it to.

great sex on the floor.

he left, i moved on and that was that.

the fact that i'm still thinking about it

tells me that feeling free rather than the dread of loss

became a goal for me in relationships.

i realized i didn't have the time or the patience

for something to feel like a loss

before it had truly begun.

i knew from then on,

i wanted that same level of emotional euphoria.

and more really great sex...

on the floor.

this or that... no, all of it

i don't answer upon recollection

rather i voice the concentration of thought

and design of passion through instinct.

it reaches down the depths of my consciousness

to return itself, a new entity.

i do not pride myself when my response is immediate

for it is that different voice for which

i barely recognize.

yet, as the layers of masks and costume disrobe,

i begin to see it again,

that thing i call my truth.

there is a divide in how we speak.

we must define ourselves in order

to enter a conversation.

if i am this… i cannot be that.

false.

if i am this… you must be that.

false.

if i am this… i cannot be that. false.

if i am this… you must be that. false.

if i am this and you are that then we can't get along.

absolutely false.

we see this all the time.

in clichés, in politics, in our history,

we are told this and that can't be friends

but why not?

why do we have to pick?

it's like the unwritten rule

that when you sit at a lunch table

on the first day of school, it is your table

for the rest of your life. why is that?

why can't i sit with my friend

who plays soccer one day and my friend

who will one day work for nasa the next?

or better yet,

why can't that be the same fucking person?

**part three:
one long
continuous
train of thought**

the veil of perception

this is the part where i ramble.

i go on and on

about things that make sense to me

and hope someone flipping the paper

maybe gets it too.

as we reconstruct our narratives,

who are we leaving behind?

what are we leaving behind?

we all have a warped sense of reality

as we can only live our own reality.

we can only sit in the exact truth that is our own, like a

chair with our name on it.

but it then becomes our responsibility

to empathize with our neighbors

and stretch beyond the bounds

that can keep us within our own tunnel of vision.

the tunnel that can entrap us in comfort.

the kind that can refuse to search for more.

our expressions are like

beads of rain on the car window,

which ones are drawn back and merge together

and which ones pass quietly

onward, alone.

what we are

and who we are

create so many questions.

i am who i am

but that is not permanent.

if it was, things would be easier to predict.

our hearts would be broken less,

our detours wouldn't exist in the first place.

we'd be the one lane road crossing

the valley of disconnect,

unwilling to try the path through

the snowy caps of boundless reaching.

my question is...

why are we so obsessed with absolutes?

is it a rooted fear of something not making sense

like if it doesn't make sense,

then nothing else matters,

like our conscious being can't go on?

when things don't make sense,

it is our obligation to seek the answer,

not submit to the finite uncertainty.

to get the answers we seek,

we have to ask the uncomfortable questions

and why wouldn't they be uncomfortable?

comfort is set in the familiar.

to learn,

is to be willingly active in the acknowledgement

of what we don't know and pursuant

in asking more questions.

that's how we grow, isn't it?

it's not what we see right now,

but what we see overall,

the gathering of information and purpose

spread into the direction of intent.

it is the past,

the future,

and the now

willing to work as one.

for the culmination of success

does not reside in one

but in the fingertips of the many.

there are some things you pick up over time

as habits, whether through one's environment

or practice.

there are things over that same period of time

that you force as habits,

enshrining their existence by pure will.

but at what point do we find change to be a part of the

natural evolution

rather than forcing the desperate push

towards changing the pendulum's swing for the sake of

the wake that one is expected to follow…

a wake of comfort.

a desire of the honored change

that encourages awareness

rather than the false narrative

that tries to pave the road

before even understanding

the earth around it

to encourage listening,

to encourage breath,

fluid into the space of our lungs,

and being that deserves

the right to exist,

deserves the right to take up that space

in the first place.

who are we in this world if we

don't think,

feel,

empathize?

we would lie flat,

unwavering on a wall of rocks,

ready to crumble at the discontent of information.

we would feel void,

lacking the depth of discovery and its

endless pursuit of tangible expression.

this growth, change, path is dynamic and full.

if we don't empathize,

we disintegrate.

and am i really that fragile?

am i really that cold?

i encourage you to ask yourself

what moves you,

who do you empathize with?

am i that unsure

that the slightest wind of indecency

could tip me over?

am i that faint

in the determination of my self-discovery,

that i pass my own reflection without a shred

of acknowledgement?

am i that adamant that change will cause me pain?

am i sure about why i feel this way?

...

did you ask yourself questions?

wonder at why you thought something all along,

without being aware to its origin

in your mind's chemistry?

i challenge myself to ask all the time and reflect on

what i feel is truly me

and make sure that i am constantly pursing

that depth, whether on the days i'm most receptive

or the days i'm most shallow,

i do not dismiss the goal

of reflection and consideration.

in it all, haven't i proven again

and again

that my strength does not conclude

in the outward appearance of brutish force

but the inward system of thought?

sometimes i picture the movie.

you know the one.

the one where we say

all the things we wish we'd said

the first time.

all the truth,

pain, and intentional slashes

on the other's ego to return the favor.

monologues of poignant words

strung together like a beaded necklace

ready to wear that crown of higher morality

and pride against the opposed.

but that movie doesn't get to happen

unless we write it ourselves.

we don't usually have the chance to tell him

your friendship was empty

the second your vows showed to be based on convenience.

to tell her

your harsh perspective wasn't yours to have

but you wanted me to bend to it

because it was somehow the most worthy perspective of all.

to tell them

my pain is not yours to use as pity

for it's the reason i could walk away in the first place.

sometimes i wish i had this movie moment.

other times i wish to never have this movie moment.

sometimes i wish for that immediate perspective

so i wouldn't have to think of the movie moment

so long after.

other times, i'm thankful for the chance to

gain perspective.

the only thing i know for sure

is whether the moment to stand up for yourself

comes back around

or not,

your acceptance of what led you here

is not dependent

on that moment's existence.

it is dependent on when you are ready to move on.

to move on in your own way

that is completely determined by you.

you need to burn an anniversary picture?

burn it.

you need to go on the hike of your dreams

to see the world from a new perspective?

go.

you need to hear the person's name

without the unsettling gnawing in your stomach?

then don't shy away from it.

believe

that it isn't only you who feels hurt,

but it is only you that gets to decide

how to heal your hurt.

and when you do...

you'll begin to morph,

adapt,

transcend the situation

and cosmic sensation of the past

into the butterflies of future endeavors.

you'll decide it's time...

to leap out of the sandbox,

past the expectations

and into who you want to be when you grow up.

part four:
transcendent
above the archaic...
(or over the bullshit)

the veil of confidence

fly girl

i want to fly

above the broken bricks of tiered city buildings

into the sweep of air that fills my lungs.

i want to fly

above the broken beliefs that i have left behind,

into the swathe of new directions and

unbridled choices.

i want to fly

above the first layer into the fabrication of

something bigger,

something more.

i will fly

above what i believed to once be true,

above what i believed to once be it,

above what is said to be and

into what can be.

sunrise with abe

i went to college in d.c.

which is a town

full of discoveries and opportunities

to expand your mind.

during my sophomore year, some friends of mine

and i decided to do sunrise at the mall.

the mall being the national mall,

not the big buildings that ruled the 90's.

we woke up at the ass crack of dawn

and made our way through the emptied d.c. streets,

the light orange glow peaking up through the still

darkened morning. the crisp morning only cluttered

with the occasional cyclist and black suv.

we went down to the mall and found parking

which in d.c. is rare.

georgetown is the worst but i digress.

we sat on the steps of the lincoln memorial

and watched the sun rise over the washington monument.

the sun climbed in the sky,

overlooking years of history.

it peaked the crest of the washington monument and

illuminated the heart of our country.

i sat in front of abe

thinking that the future held the breadth of opportunity.

i chose to do something uncharacteristic of my usual

day to day by waking up early and getting downtown.

it seems simple but that moment

gave me such perspective.

i chose this.

i chose change.

i chose experience.

i was sitting in the city that held so many moments.

and i was choosing to be a part of them.

even as the cold stone started to etch

its way through my clothes to my

winter-chilled skin,

i appreciated it and felt alive.

change has become somewhat addictive for me.

i need it.

i crave it.

i change my room fifty times and shuffle my organization

around me. thats when i feel relaxed.

only now can i understand the impact of a

seemingly small choice,

to wake up early and sit with abe

but it gave me so much.

it gave me a taste of the unexpected that i was

unknowingly hinged upon, the adventure that my body

ached for and my creative mind longed to be a part of.

i was not stagnant as i had up to this point so often felt.

through the eating disorders and ongoing recovery,

the mental health ups and down and the desperate change

of schools to find seemingly stable ground,

i feared becoming unloveable,

unmoving and stale.

like the creativity and inspiration would be sucked

from my neck by the vampire called fear.

that's fear with a capital f...

one of the worst f words.

that moment showed me, like the sun rising,

that i was moving.

toward something still unknown...

which maybe was the best part.

archaic

to feel alive what do we need?

a pinch on the arm, or the beckoning of a love

aroused in the encircling energy that comes from

experience.

it latches onto me and gives me the chance to take hold.

i grip this opportunity like the steering wheel of a car

headed into the unknown only severed

by a lack of trust in

myself.

to feel alive what do we need?

hot coals under our feet or the sensation of shoes that won't

bend to our tread,

the tongue of another encircled in ours,

the embrace that pushes against our skin and

presses our nerves into submission and then

pain free existence?

to feel alive what do i need?

freedom to make choices,

left of the abrupt nature

i find when i don't listen to the voice in my head,

pushing past the effete into the tangibly real,

griping onto whatever stimulates my creativity,

blowing past reality,

into the subconscious needs,

i sense the visceral of my dream.

i've never been one to ask for permission

for things i want to go do or create myself

but i found i ask permission for other things,

things that are small

as if i need approval to do them.

i was once awarded a "questioner award" at camp.

at first i was embarrassed,

offended at such a weird superlative

but then i realized that it didn't mean asking questions to

be annoying. it was about being inquisitive.

wanting to know what

and how

and why

so that my day to day existence was rooted

in tangible idiosyncrasies that made it

real.

made it a place of growth not a

place of passive observance.

i do not want what i can't have,

i'm told not to be unless i've already been,

to stay calm in the face of everything,

those are the realities of a super mortal

but what,

what if i am not super?

my mortality is the thing i hold most precious,

tender and strong simultaneously,

that is a power to witness.

so what,

what is my responsibility as a mere mortal?

to be something i've never been

because i can?

to do something because i tell myself

i can

not because i am waiting for the permission of others

but because i give permission onto myself.

next, i don't know which steps to take.

but that is the idea of mortality.

the steps i forge into the transient field in front of me

are mine to choose,

mine to sketch,

mine to imprint into this existence as my doing.

yet what do i see here?

a fresh start,

a new beginning,

or my imagination expanding to encompass it all

the old,

the new,

the now.

creases

old enough to feel

too young as to not be wise enough to understand.

that in-between can feel as broad as the ocean.

there is never an island big enough to stay

and never a wave small enough to pretend it doesn't exist.

how do we see age?

as the forgiveness for us to continue to be accepted by

others as if those waves were our fault

and we left those islands on purpose?

age is a sketch.

a sketch on the top soil of our expression

we are expected to smooth the soil over and over again,

weighing down the particles of the nutrient rich

reimagining the landscape to be less seemingly abrasive,

decorating the uneven land to barely recognize it.

what else do we erase?

experience,

expression,

honesty,

time?

as if larger notions that are out of our control

always mean antagonistic responses.

sketch experience.

the time we take to learn

or the money we invest to know,

the names we are informed by

and the repetition we are not to make.

sketch expression.

what i dare not hide

so that i don't slowly deceive myself

into being another.

sketch honesty.

for if we try to erase it

what are we left with?

sketch time.

the time you plan for,

the time you want to have,

and the time you are living

right now.

to erase it,

is to miss what is happening right in front of us.

lines are dynamic.

we want to assume they are linear

as their names proclaim

but what is a line that

does not bend?

a graph,

pavement,

a lie,

something unwilling to adjust,

unwilling to learn,

unwilling to empathize?

lines are powerful tools

to encircle,

to trace,

to find new visions on the blank canvas that we were given.

many times, i tried to start over

thinking it was the only way.

leave a toxic relationship

or walk away from a situation

that was rooted in indifference.

but what we really do when we start over

is redraw ourselves.

and those sketches are not effervescent.

they seep into the pages below,

into the back cover of the sketchbook that has been there

all along.

those pages can be torn,

pulled and yanked from their coil

but subtly embedded in the fibers of reshaped trees

are the reminiscent lines of the sketch that came before it.

we grow.

lines grow and morph into shapes.

how are we any different?

if i stopped to think about my own growth,

this book would go on forever.

we can't be linear in the traditional form

without missing out on the chance to grow.

we need it.

we crave it

like the uncontrollable sugar drool that surprises us

every time we smell a sweet ice cream shop.

it's when we don't grow,

we don't crave that we should ask ourselves why?

why are we only accepting and not pursuing?

what have we let go of?

what do we want?

nude beach

i've traveled many places and to a nude beach.

yes, this is where my european anecdote will begin.

i was in santorini with two other women

and we heard of this nude beach.

now, i'm not unaware.

i know they exist but they're not a thing in the u.s.

unless you know something because if so

you need to tell me!

so we decide we must go and experience this.

the nude beach on the island,

surrounded by the aegean blue

that is just impeccable.

the local cab takes us to the edge of a field

on the edge of the island.

it is secluded on its own,

with the black cliffs and green shrubbery surrounding us.

we walk through this field,

the path is barely identifiable between the rock and sand

that littered the grass.

it leads us to the beach.

a small exit by the immediate looks of it.

then, we turn and tucked in the concave cliffs

was a nude beach.

not large but secluded.

the black sand was expansive as if a paved runway

towards the few naked people that spattered the way.

the thing was... i didn't feel unsafe.

i wasn't self-conscious or insecure.

the thing that struck me was that i was prepared

to feel unsafe.

i expected it.

that's what i am trained to feel.

the hair on the back of my neck,

the fear of a camera lens,

or the leers that last longer than they should.

yet, i didn't.

i let the grecian surrounding comfort me,

hold me in the warmth of the ancient earth

and remember that feeling as it should be,

a more frequent part of my day,

the freedom to be in existence as i am.

fraud

i've felt like a fraud my entire life,

never enough to qualify for one thing,

to attain the specific accolades that would

render me worthy to everyone else.

what we see and what we are,

two different things often made to be one.

i am worthy.

yet to be told you're not enough,

it's a statement with the weight to

crumble a forest into splintered

pieces of forgotten ecosystems

for my worth is not tied to yours.

the chain of your wrecking ball wants to loop us in and

hold onto the expectations that you have set

for those are how you need to see things

to make sense of the world.

but that's not how i see things.

i thrive from variety,

the empathy that courses through

the cells of beings

into the furthest

memories of my mind.

enough is not a specified measurement

so who are you to determine its bounds?

for to determine the width of an emotional box

someone is to stay in

is the cruelest of friendships.

that's not a true friend

but a false friend comforted

by someone else's limitations.

i am enough.

what i define as enough is within my grasp.

it molds, evolves and

finds a euphoric sense of self

in an everyday discovery.

and i will not let someone else

put onto me a definition that makes them

more comfortable.

i am enough.

the way back

how do we see forever?

something concrete,

something stained into the epidermis of our life

like a tattoo.

why do we put onto ourselves

that which cannot be easily changed?

do we like the challenge,

the intensity

or the intimacy that comes with a choice

of something forever ours to behold?

we do not drift from a tattoo.

it is within our skin,

needles made sure of that.

the image of our visceral emotion

there for us to remember.

tattoos hold the desired weight.

like they can be traced by the finger of a lover

but never wiped away.

permeance is a tricky concept.

why do we chose permanent things?

we wish for something to sustain us?

we like the immensity of what we have chosen?

why do tattoos become the immediate symbol

of permeant things?

maybe it's the choice we have to get them

or the idea that they are externalizations

of what we feel that is permanently already

within us.

so not everything is permanent or a tattoo.

would you rather fix it

or keep what you have learned from your mistake?

of course we'd do things differently

if we could go back.

that's the point of learning

and growing.

it doesn't mean we have to regret

the things we'd change just have a different appreciation

of what we learned from them.

regret is wasted energy more often than not.

wasted on time

we can't turn back,

on decisions we can't undo

rather than put into the future

of perception undutifully keeping aware of itself.

what time i've wasted on fear,

on regret

or the scripted narrative in my head of how

i would have handled the situation differently.

but isn't that a common notion?

that we desire to change that last relationship,

exam gone wrong

or text message sent to the wrong person,

that we are encumbered with understanding,

that our decisions and actions have consequences,

to learn that before the consequences run much deeper.

i can't pretend that i don't still feel pain

from those i feel have wronged me

but they don't care about that do they?

their journey and my own were intertwined so briefly

as if an accidental brush of a strangers hand

that to assume consideration

or anything from them is a wave of energy lost

to the massive sea of discontent.

i cannot waste my energy.

my energy stems from many things,

from the raging fire that is my passion,

from the ever present empathy that drives my creativity,

from the stream of consciousness

that gives me poetic notion

in the most self-centered of times,

from the wall that i set in front of myself

only to push my climb that much higher,

from the vaults that encompass the larger me,

the me that is more complex

than the one dimensional image,

from the support that i am gifted to be able to have,

from the notion that the breath i take is mine

to do with as i please

to let it fuel my body at its molecular level,

feeding my mind and my heart to share joy and

consideration to give nutrients to the muscles

that tell me i can handle a day at a time,

from the idea that the next drink

i pour is mine to choose,

to sip

and appreciate,

for the idea

that i am high maintenance and

proud of the internal diversity

that gives me the ability

to empathize and listen and heal.

my energy comes from me

and that is enough.

in fact, it's more than enough.

to all the people asking...

please stop.

don't ask me why i don't want kids.

don't ask me why i think i won't change my mind.

don't ask me if i'm dating anyone.

don't ask me if i am lonely.

if i know you well enough,

then you'll get your answer when its time

and i will let you know when that time is.

i'm not offended when people i know

ask me about my personal life.

it's my choice to tell them the answer

if i trust they can hold the truth

with respect.

it's when those that i don't know

or who really don't know me

ask.

and ask me

and ask me again

expecting a different answer

like my response is a reaction

based on whether or not i've eaten recently.

these questions aren't inherently rude.

what's rude is expecting a certain response

before i open my mouth.

the ending... no, the beginning

overall, what i know

is you can be more than one thing.

you have to be determined and focused

because we can truly only do so much in one day...

yet,

we can also do so much in one day

because i will not box myself in absolutes.

the things i've done despite what i've been through,

the things i've done because of my support system,

the things i've done at my worst,

the things i've done because i chose to.

yea,

they all make sense.

the habits and practice

or forced habits of will.

which is most powerful?

which is most powerful now

versus the long run?

you can be more than one thing.

your path does not have to have the bounds at which

others materialize.

it is not a maze made of hay for the walls to feel impossibly

high and unwilling to move without disaster.

release those constraints or

take a sledgehammer to those walls if you must

or try not to put on the weights of others

in the first place.

because the only blanket statement i know is that

your path,

your true course,

your motto or through-line

is you.